Living Nature

BIRDS

Chrysalis Children's Books

The publishers wish to thank the following for permission to reproduce copyright material:

Oxford Scientific Films and individual copyright holders on the following pages: Doug Allan 4, 7, Rafi Ben-Shahar 5, Raymond Blythe 24, Roger Brown 23, Martyn Chillmaid 9, John Downer 28/29, Michael Fogden 19, Bob Frederick 7, Arthur Gloor/Animals animals 19, Philippe Henry 14, Michael Leach 15, Roland Mayr 22, 23, Patti Murray/Animals Animals 4, Alan G Nelson/Animals Animals 1, Ben Osborne 9, 17, Stan Osolinski cover, 3, 6/7, 8, 25, Richard Packwood 24, 27, Peter Parks 24, C M Perrins 27, Hans Reinhard/Okapia 10, 16, Leonard Lee Rue III/Animals Animals 11, Alastair Shay 5, Tony Tilford 11, 12/13.

This edition published in 2003 by
Chrysalis Children's Books
The Chrysalis Building, Bramley Rd,
London W10 6SP

Photographs copyright © Oxford Scientific Films and individual copyright holders
Format and illustrations © Chrysalis Books PLC

Printed in Hong Kong

ISBN 1 84138 628 6

British Library Cataloguing in Publication Data CIP data for this book is available from the British Library

A Belitha Book

Editor: Serpentine Editorial
Series designer: Frances McKay
Consultant: Andrew Branson

Words in **bold** are in the glossary on page 30

Title page picture: A hummingbird hovers in front of a flower to feed on the sugary nectar inside.

Contents page picture: this is a saddleback stork which comes from Africa.

Contents

What is a bird?

You might think that a bird is an animal that has wings and can fly. But some birds, such as penguins and ostriches, cannot fly, while bats and insects can fly but are not birds.

▼ Penguins live in Antarctica. This penguin chick is eating fish from its parent's beak.

▼ Flamingoes live on lakes and **marshes** in Africa. They use their long necks to dip their beaks into the water to search for food.

Birds are the only animals that have feathers, and all birds have them. This book shows many kinds of birds, from all around the world. They vary in size, and have different-shaped wings and beaks to suit the different ways they live.

▼ Ostriches live on the grassy plains of Africa. They are taller than a person, and are the biggest birds in the world. Ostriches cannot fly but they can run faster than people.

▼ Parrots have bright colourful feathers. They eat fruit and flowers and live in large, noisy groups in tropical forests.

Feathers

Feathers keep a bird warm and dry, and help it to fly. A bird has two main kinds of feathers. The outer feathers are called contour feathers. They give the bird its particular markings.

Underneath are soft, fluffy down feathers. They lie next to the bird's skin and help to keep the bird warm

▶ Birds have extra long feathers on their wings and tails. This bird is drying its wings in the sun.

▲ Outer feathers overlap each other to make a watertight covering over the bird's skin.

▲ Like all young birds, penguin chicks have only down feathers. Outer feathers will grow later.

▼ Outer feathers are flat and smooth. Down feathers are soft and fluffy. The close-up shows how the outer feathers are held together by tiny hooks.

Looking after feathers

Birds need to keep their feathers clean and tidy. If they become ragged they do not work so well. Birds use the edge of their beaks to **preen** their feathers. Preening gets rid of dirt and makes sure that all the tiny hooks are joined together.

▼ A heron uses its long beak to clean its feathers. It pulls them through its beak to comb out the tangles and to remove the dirt.

Did you know?
Some swans have more than 25,000 feathers to preen.

As a bird preens, it covers its feathers with oil to keep them soft and waterproof. The oil comes from a special preen **gland** near the tail. Birds lose and regrow their feathers.

▼ These goose feathers are so well oiled the water just rolls off them.

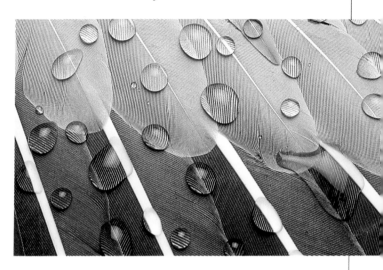

▶ This young albatross has started to lose the soft downy feathers it was born with. Soon it will grow bigger, adult feathers.

Eye-catching

Many male birds have brightly-coloured feathers, although few can match the wonderful feathers of the male bird of paradise. The male birds use their bright feathers to attract a female. Females and chicks are usually dull and drab compared with the males so they can remain hidden in the trees.

The male bird of paradise has a colourful tail.

Females need to hide because they have to sit on the nest to hatch eggs. They do not want to be seen by hunting animals. The chicks, too, are in danger until they can fly.

▼ This chick is a wild turkey. The colour of its feathers make the chick hard to see among the dead leaves.

▼ Both of these birds are purple honeycreepers, but only the male bird is purple. The female's feathers make her hard to see among the trees.

How to fly

Most birds can fly, except for penguins, ostriches and a few others. To see how a bird flies, take a piece of paper and hold one end in front of your mouth. Blow hard across the top of the paper. The paper should start to flutter upwards.

▼ Then the robin moves its wings back to push itself up and forwards.

▲ As the robin flaps its wings, it moves them down.

▼ A bird's wing is curved to give it more lift. Air flows faster over the top than underneath, helping the bird to rise.

Did you know?

The wandering albatross has the largest wingspan. Its wings are 3.5 metres from tip to tip.

▼ When the wings point downwards, the feathers close together and the wings push the robin forwards.

▼ When the wings point upwards, the feathers part and let air through them.

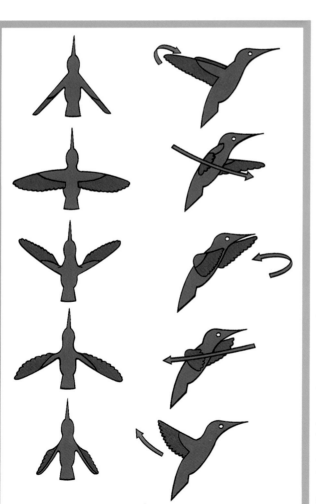

◄ A hummingbird is like a helicopter. It can fly forwards, backwards, and even hover in one spot. It does so by tilting, turning and twisting its wings.

When a bird flies, the air passing over the top of the wing moves more quickly than air caught under the wing. This means there is more **pressure** under the wing, and the bird is pushed up.

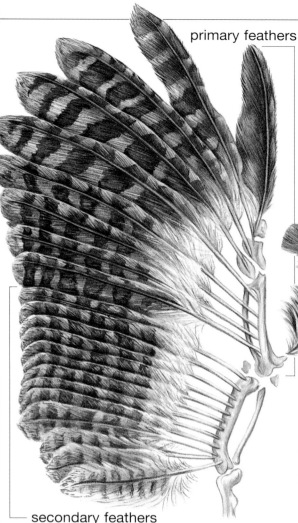

primary feathers

secondary feathers

Flying machine

A bird has two kinds of wing feathers. Large primary feathers push the bird through the air. The secondary feathers make a smooth surface for the air to flow over.

◀ Feathers grow out of the bones of the wings. The largest feathers, the primary feathers, are at the wingtips.

▼Swans are big and heavy. Their huge chest muscles work hard as they take off.

Did you know?

Swifts love to fly. They can fly for up to two years without a break, feeding and sleeping in mid air.

▲ This white dove is landing. It is using the power of its muscles to control its wings and tail.

A bird needs to be strong but light to fly. It has large, powerful **muscles** in its chest to move its wings, and its bones are light and hollow. Some birds' bones are lighter than their feathers.

15

Wing shapes

The shape of a bird's wings suits the kind of life the bird leads. Birds that live in woods and forests usually have short, blunt wings to fly from tree to tree.

But some birds can fly without flapping their wings very much.

◀ An owl's wings feel like velvet. They make no noise as the owl flies through the dark, hunting for food.

Eagles and owls soar above the ground on broad wings, while seabirds glide on long thin wings. Even flightless birds use their wings. An ostrich's wings help the bird to balance as it runs. Penguins use their wings as paddles to help them swim.

▲ An eagle soars high above the ground. It does not have to move its wings much because it is riding on a warm current of air.

▼ An albatross glides on the wind over the ocean. Its long, narrow wings point backwards to make them more **streamlined**.

▼ As the sun heats the land, warm air rises up making the air currents the birds ride on.

Beaks

A bird uses its beak to pick up food, to build a nest, and to clean, or preen, itself (see page 8). A beak is hard and strong but, because a bird has no teeth, it cannot chew its food. Food is ground up in a kind of second stomach called a **gizzard** instead.

▶ A toucan's huge beak looks heavy and clumsy, but it isn't. Toucans can pick up tiny berries in their giant beaks. They use their beaks like knives to slice up soft, juicy fruits.

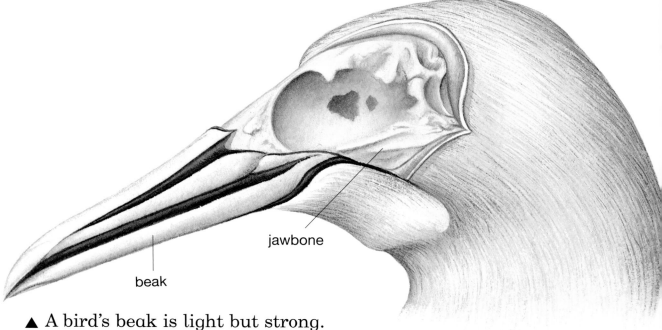

jawbone

beak

▲ A bird's beak is light but strong. It is made of a horny substance that covers the bird's jaw bones.

▼ A weaver uses its feet to make a nest.

Beak shapes

The birds shown here all have differently shaped beaks because they eat different kinds of food. They also have different ways of catching their food. **Birds of prey**, such as hawks and owls, swoop down on their prey and snatch it in their claws. Seed-eaters fly from one plant to the next to feed.

▲ A goshawk hunts other birds and small animals. It has a hooked beak for tearing apart its **prey**.

◀ A hawfinch likes to eat cherry stones. It crushes them in its short, strong beak.

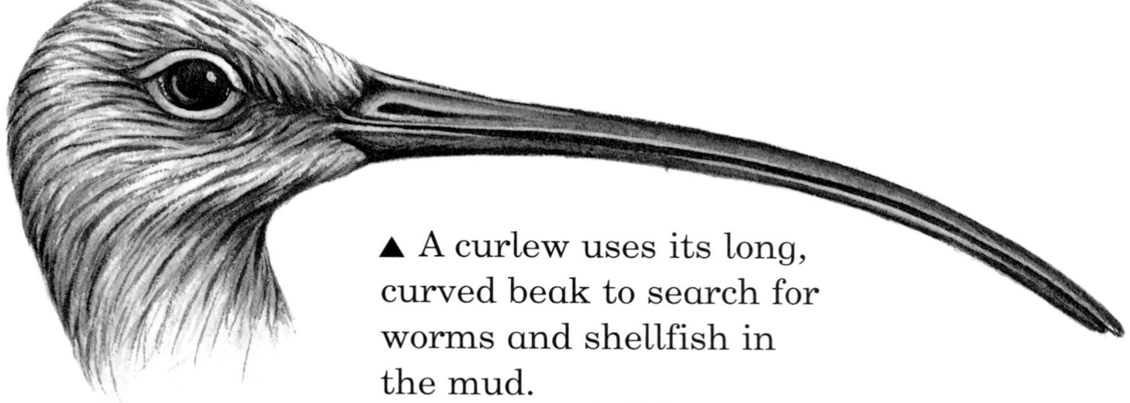

▲ A curlew uses its long, curved beak to search for worms and shellfish in the mud.

▶ Ducks strain the pond water through their flat beaks to find food. This shoveler duck has a particularly wide beak shaped like a spade or shovel.

Herons and pelicans are experts at catching fish. Herons use their dagger-like bills to grab fish, but pelicans scoop them into their pouches. Curlews and some ducks stick their beaks into mud, searching for food.

▶ A pelican can catch several fish in the stretchy pouch of skin under its beak.

Did you know?

The pelican's beak is the longest in the world. Some are over 45 cm long – about as long as your arm. The beak is about one third of the length of the pelican.

Bird songs

A reed warbler singing loudly.

Many birds are superb singers. Male birds often sing in spring when they are looking for a **mate**. Even when he has found a mate, the male carries on singing to tell other birds to keep away from his **territory** and the nest.

Males and females also use short calls. A sharp call warns other birds of danger – a cat, perhaps, or a bird of prey. Birds that live in flocks call to each other to keep in touch. In the same way parents call to their young.

▶ A bittern 'booms' rather than sings. It sounds a bit like a ship's foghorn and can be heard several kilometres away.

Did you know?

A reed warbler is an amazing singer. It can sing two different tunes at once.

▼ These tree ducks usually feed in thick reeds where they cannot see each other. They whistle so that the whole group can keep together.

Eggs and nests

Some birds build a nest of twigs, grass and feathers. Others simply lay their eggs in a dip in the ground. Birds sit on their eggs to keep them warm. A tiny chick grows inside each egg.

▼ The tiny red blob at the centre of this egg is a chick. It grows inside the shell for three weeks.

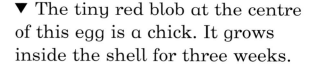

▲ This blackbird chick is the first in the nest to **hatch** out of its egg.

◀ When a chick is ready to hatch, it starts to peck a hole in the shell. As soon as the hole is big enough, the chick slowly pushes and pulls itself out.

The growing chick feeds on the yellow yolk. It breathes in air through tiny holes in the hard shell. The clear egg white protects the chick from bumps and knocks.

▶ Newborn albatross chicks are helpless. They stay in the nest and their mother brings them food. After a few weeks, the chicks are big and strong enough to learn to fly.

Egg shapes

Birds' eggs vary in colour, shape and size. Some blend in with the background. A tern's eggs look like pebbles on the ground. An osprey's eggs look like tree bark. Birds that nest in dark holes have round, white eggs.

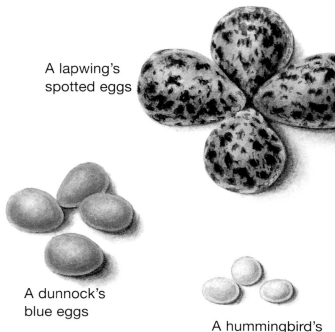

A lapwing's spotted eggs

A dunnock's blue eggs

A hummingbird's tiny eggs

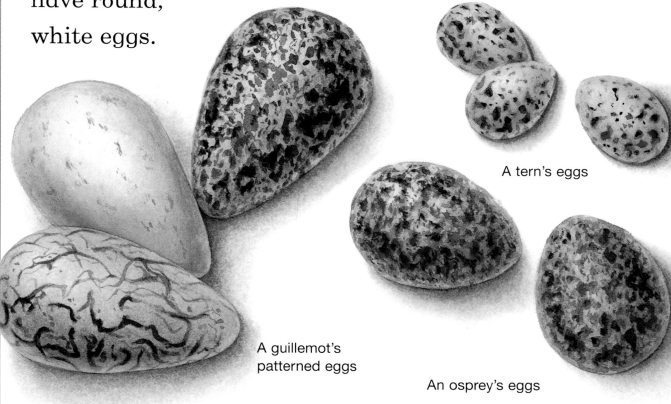

A tern's eggs

A guillemot's patterned eggs

An osprey's eggs

Small birds lay small eggs. The eggs of a hummingbird are as small as your thumbnail. Large birds lay large eggs. The biggest of all is an ostrich egg, which weighs as much as 40 hen's eggs.

▲ A tawny owl builds its nest in a deep hole in a tree. The eggs are white so that the owl can see them in the dark.

▼Guillemots' eggs are specially shaped to stop them rolling off the cliffs into the sea. Instead of rolling, they spin in a circle.

World of birds

There are about 9000 different kinds of birds. They live in different kinds of places – in forests, on lakes, in towns, and by the sea, even in the icy Arctic. Some birds **migrate** from one place to another. Barnacle geese, for example, spend the summer in the Arctic, but fly south for the winter.

▶ Geese usually fly in small family groups. They are led by the older, stronger female birds.

Some birds live on their own. Others live in **flocks** or large **colonies**. Their beaks, wings and even their eggs are shaped to suit the way they live.

Glossary

Bird of prey A bird that hunts other birds and animals for its food. Eagles, hawks and owls are all birds of prey.

Colony A large group of birds or animals of the same kind that live together.

Flock A large group of birds.

Gland Part of the body which produces a special substance. A preen gland produces oil.

Gizzard A kind of second stomach which only birds have. Birds have no teeth, so the gizzard has strong muscles to do the job instead. Birds often eat small stones to help the gizzard grind up their food.

Hatch A chick hatches when it breaks out of the egg. Hatching can take several hours and is very exhausting for the young chick.

Marshes Low, wet land which is partly flooded with water.

Mate One of a pair of birds – one male, one female – who together produce and raise young birds.

Migrate To fly or travel from one place to another a long way away, to live there for part of the year. Some kinds of birds and animals migrate to avoid bad weather or to find food in winter.

Muscles Meaty substance inside the body which make the bones and various other parts of the body move.

Preen To keep feathers clean and tidy. The outer feathers are held together by tiny hooks. Preening rejoins the hooks and keeps the feathers airtight.

Pressure Force which presses on a surface. Air pressure is the force of the atmosphere (the air above the earth) 'pressing down'.

Prey Animal or bird which is hunted by other animals or birds for food.

Streamlined Shaped to move easily and smoothly through air or water.

Territory An area that a bird lives in and where it finds its food. An animal defends its territory against other animals of the same kind.

Key facts

Largest bird Ostriches are the tallest birds. Some are up to 2.4 metres tall and can weigh as much as 140 kilograms. Compare this with an average adult man, who measures just 1.75 metres and weighs about 76 kilograms.

Heaviest flying bird The heaviest bird to get off the ground is probably the Kori bustard which weighs up to 18 kilograms, about one eighth the weight of the flightless ostrich.

Smallest bird The bee hummingbird is less than 6 cm long and half of that is its beak and tail. The bee humming-bird's body is about half the length of your little finger.

Fastest flier Swifts can fly straight forwards at up to 100 kilometres an hour – nearly as fast as traffic on a motorway. But a peregrine falcon can dive on to its prey at up to 250 kilometres an hour. It could dive to the ground from the top of the Eiffel Tower in just 4 seconds.

Most travelled The Arctic tern migrates from the North Pole to the South Pole and back again each year. It flies about 40,000 kilometres and sees more sunlight than any other animal.

Most common bird There are about 3000 million hens in the world out of a total of 100,000 million birds. The most common wild bird is the red-billed quelea which lives in Africa. There are about 10,000 million of them.

Fastest wingbeat One kind of hummingbird, the horned sungem, can beat its wings an amazing 90 times a second.

Weight lifters Eagles can snatch and carry in their talons animals weighing as much as 9 kilograms.

Earliest bird The earliest known bird was archeopteryx, which lived about 150 million years ago, at the same time as the dinosaurs.

Index

EDUCATION LIBRARY SERVICE

Browning Way
Woodford Park Industrial Estate
Winsford
Cheshire CW7 2JN

Phone: 01606 592551/557126
Fax: 01606 861412
www.cheshire.gov.uk/els/home.htm

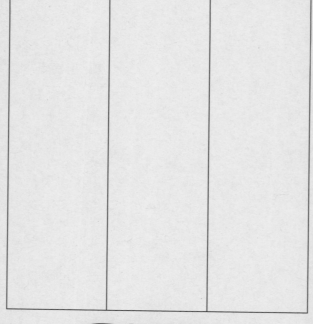

CHESHIRE
COUNTY COUNCIL